T JOKES EVERY 10 YEAR OLD SHOULD KNOW

FUNNY KIDS JOKES

TO MAKE YOU LAUGH

HOLLI & EVAN WHALING

∽ DEDICATION ∽

This book is dedicated to
Our WhalePod: Mike, Ev & Ace.

Laughing together with you
Makes every day better!

when in doubt,
Always choose joy.

Love,
Mom

TABLE OF CONTENTS

INTRODUCTION

Hey there kids! Do you like jokes? Looking for some jokes that are sure to make you giggle? We sure do! And today is your lucky day! Look no further than this really funny book of jokes that's perfect for 10-year-olds. If you're not 10 yet, don't worry – this book is still for you!

We love jokes in our house, and we collected some of our favorites to share with you! There are jokes about nature, animals, school, teachers, and even middle schoolers! This book has knock-knock jokes to have you rolling on the floor laughing and one-liners to make your parents' eyes roll!

Have a long car ride coming up? Need to cheer up a friend? Want to be the star of the talent show? Keep this book handy, and you'll always be able to entertain yourself or a friend!

These silly, goofy jokes are sure to make you laugh. So why not give them a try today?

So sit back, relax, and get ready to laugh your socks off!

Chapter 1: FOOD Jokes

The first chapter
has the best 16 food jokes
to make meal time more fun

WHAT DO YOU CALL A SAD STRAWBERRY?

A blueberry!

WHAT FRUIT TEASES PEOPLE A LOT?

Ba-na, na, na, na...na!

WHAT DO YOU CALL TWO BANANA PEELS?

A pair of slippers!

HOW DO YOU MAKE GOLD SOUP?

Put in 14 carrots.

WHAT DO YOU CALL A PISTACHIO ON A SPACESHIP?

An astro-nut!

WHAT SOUND DOES A NUT MAKE WHEN IT SNEEZES?

Ca-shew!

TWO PICKLES FELL OUT OF A JAR ONTO THE FLOOR. WHAT DID ONE SAY TO THE OTHER?

Dill with it

WHAT DO YOU CALL A SHOE MADE FROM A BANANA?

A Slipper

WHAT DO YOU CALL A SWEET POTATO ON THE HIGHWAY?

A traffic yam

WHAT KIND OF NUT HAS NO SHELL?

Doughnut

WHAT DO YOU GIVE
A SICK LEMON?

Lemon Aid

WHAT DID THE TOMATO SAY
TO THE KETCHUP BOTTLE?

How you doin' brother.

WHAT DID THE REPORTER SAY TO THE ICE CREAM?

What's the scoop?

HOW DOES A CUCUMBER BECOME A PICKLE?

It goes through a jarring experience.

HOW DID THE LETTUCE BEAT THE CARROT IN A MIDDLE SCHOOL TRACK MEET?

Because it was a head!

WHAT DO YOU CALL A MONKEY THAT LOVES POTATO CHIPS?

A chipmunk

CHAPTER 2: ANIMAL JOKES

This chapter
has the best 60 funny
Animal jokes

WHY DO DUCKS MAKE GOOD DETECTIVES?

They always quack the case

WHAT DID THE FISH SAY WHEN HE SWAM INTO A WALL?

Dam

WHAT PART OF A FISH WEIGHS THE MOST?

The scales!

WHAT DO YOU CALL A HIPPO WITH A MESSY ROOM?

A hippopota mess!

HOW DO BEES BRUSH THEIR HAIR?

They use honeycombs

WHAT DO YOU CALL A DEER WITH NO EYES?

No eye deer

WHAT DO YOU CALL A DINOSAUR WITH A EXTENSIVE VOCABULARY?

A thesaurus.

WHAT DID THE LLAMA SAY WHEN HE GOT KICKED OUT OF THE ZOO?

"Alpaca my bags!"

WHERE DOES A KILLER WHALE GO FOR BRACES?

The orca-dontist.

WHAT DO YOU CALL A SHEEP COVERED IN CHOCOLATE?

A candy baaa

WHY DID THE LION SPIT OUT THE CLOWN?

Because he tasted funny

HOW DO YOU STOP A BULL FROM CHARGING?

Take away its credit cards

WHAT DO YOU CALL A DINOSAUR FART?

A blast from the past.

WHY CAN'T YOU SEND A DUCK TO SPACE?

Because the bill would be astronomical

WHAT'S A CAT'S FAVORITE MAGAZINE?

A cat-alogue.

WHAT DID THE MAMA COW SAY TO THE CALF?

It's pasture bedtime!

WHAT IS A PONY'S FAVORITE JUICE?

lemon-neigh'd.

WHAT KIND OF KEY CAN NEVER UNLOCK A DOOR?

A Monkey

WHY DON'T SHARKS EAT CLOWNS?

Because they taste funny.

WHAT IS A COW WITHOUT A MAP?

Udderly Lost

WHERE DO ORCAS HEAR MUSIC?

Orca-stras

HOW DOES A SQUID GO INTO BATTLE?

Well Armed

WHAT DO POLAR BEARS EAT FOR LUNCH?

Ice bergers

WHY CAN'T HUMANS HEAR A DOG WHISTLE?

Because dogs can't whistle.

WHY DID THE ROOSTER CROSS THE ROAD?

To show everyone he wasn't chicken!

WHAT'S THE DIFFERENCE BETWEEN A CAT AND A FROG?

Well, a cat has nine lives, but a frog croaks every night!

WHAT HAPPENED WHEN THE LION ATE THE COMEDIAN?

He felt funny!

TODAY I LEARNED HUMANS EAT MORE BANANAS THAN MONKEYS.

I can't remember the last time I ate a monkey.

WHAT IS THE EASIEST WAY TO COUNT A HERD OF COWS?

Use a cow-culator

WHY DID THE ELEPHANTS GET KICKED OUT OF THE PUBLIC POOL?

They kept dropping their trunks.

WHY DO COWS LIKE BEING TOLD JOKES?

Because they like being a-mooooosed!

WHAT DO YOU SAY IF YOU MEET A TOAD?

Wart's new?

WHAT DO YOU CALL AN ALLIGATOR IN A VEST?

An investigator!

WHAT IS THE EASIEST WAY TO COUNT A HERD OF COWS?

Get an A-Cow-tant

WHAT DO DUCKS WATCH ON TV?

Duck-umentaries

WHAT KIND OF BEE CAN'T MAKE UP ITS MIND?

A maybe

WHAT KIND OF BONE SHOULD A DOG NEVER EAT?

A trombone.

WHAT DO YOU CALL TWO BIRDS THAT ARE STUCK TOGETHER?

Vel-crows

WHERE DID THE SHEEP GO ON VACATION?

The baaaahamas

WHAT GOES TICK-TOCK AND WOOF-WOOF?

A Watchdog

WHAT DO YOU GET WHEN DINOSAURS CRASH THEIR CARS?

Tyrannosaurus wrecks.

WHAT DO YOU CALL A PILE OF KITTENS?

A meowntain.

HOW DOES A DOG STOP A VIDEO?

By hitting the paws button!

WHAT KIND OF HAIRCUTS DO BEES GET?

Buzzzzcuts!

WHAT HAPPENS TO A FROG'S CAR WHEN IT BREAKS DOWN?

It gets toad away.

WHAT IS A CROCODILE'S FAVORITE DRINK?

Gator-ade

WHAT IS A FROG'S FAVORITE RESTAURANT?

IHOP

WHAT DO YOU CALL TWO MONKEYS SHARING AN AMAZON ACCOUNT?

Prime-mates

WHY ARE BABY GOATS CALLED KIDS?

Because they're always looking for their maaaa

WHAT ANIMAL IS ALWAYS AT A BASEBALL GAME?

A bat

HOW DO YOU KNOW WHEN A DUCK HITS ITS TEEN YEARS?

Voice quacks.

WHAT DO YOU CALL A DOG IN SUMMER?

A hot dog.

WHAT DID THE FULL GLASS SAY TO THE EMPTY GLASS?

You look drunk

WHAT DO YOU CALL A COW WITH THREE LEGS?

Lean beef.

WHO DELIVERS PRESENTS TO BABY SHARKS AT CHRISTMAS?

Santa Jaws!

WHAT DO A CHICKEN AND A SCHOOL BAND HAVE IN COMMON?

They both have drum sticks!

WHAT DO YOU CALL THE HORSE THAT LIVES NEXT DOOR?

Your neighbor!

WHY ARE ELEPHANTS SO WRINKLED?

Because they take too long to iron!

WHAT DO YOU GET
WHEN YOU CROSS
AN ELEPHANT AND
A POTATO?

Mashed potato.

HOW TO BEARS KEEP COOL?

They use bear-conditioning

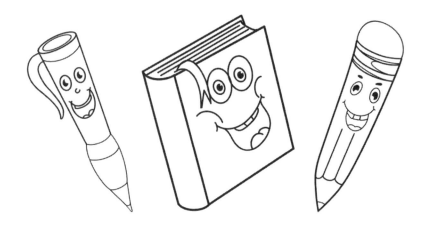

Chapter 3: SCHOOL LIFE Jokes

This chapter
has the best 20 funny
School life jokes

WHAT DID THE SCIENCE BOOK SAY TO THE MATH BOOK?

You've got problems

WHY CAN'T YOU TRUST AN ATOM?

Because they make up everything

WHAT DO YOU CALL A TEACHER WHO'S ALWAYS LATE?

Mister Bus

WHAT IS 47 + 11 + 82 + 161 + 99 + 5?

A headache

WHY WAS THE TEXTBOOK IN THE HOSPITAL?

Because it hurt its spine.

WHAT'S A TEACHER'S FAVORITE NATION?

Expla-nation.

WHAT DO YOU DO
IF THERE IS A KIDNAPPING
AT HIGH SCHOOL?

You wake him up.

DID YOU HEAR ABOUT THE
TEACHER WHO'S AFRAID OF
NEGATIVE NUMBERS?

He'll stop at nothing
to avoid them.

WHAT DO YOU CALL A MIDDLE SCHOOL STUDENT WITH CARROTS IN ITS EARS?

Anything you want,
they can't hear you!

WHY SHOULDN'T YOU TELL THE JOKE ABOUT THE CEILING TO A MIDDLE SCHOOL STUDENT?

It's way over his / her head.

WHAT TOOL DO MATH TEACHERS USE THE MOST?

Multi-pliers

WHAT STATE HAS THE LOUDEST THIRD GRADERS?

ILL-I-NOISE!

WHY WAS THE MIDDLE SCHOOL TRASHCAN SAD?

They were dumped

DID YOU HEAR ABOUT THE KIDNAPPING AT THE LOCAL MIDDLE SCHOOL?

don't worry, they woke him up.

WHY DID THE BOY BRING A LADDER TO SCHOOL?

Because he wanted to go to high school.

WHY DID THE MIDDLE SCHOOL STUDENT STARE AT THE AUTOMOBILE'S RADIO?

He wanted to watch a car-tune.

WHY DID THE HOME ECONOMICS STUDENT THROW THE BUTTER OUT THE WINDOW?

To see a butterfly!

WHAT SPELLING WORD IS ALWAYS SPELLED INCORRECTLY?

Incorrect

WHY DID THE ECHO GET DETENTION?

For answering back, back, back!

PUPIL: Sir, would you punish me for something I didn't do?

TEACHER: Of course not.

PUPIL: Good, because I didn't do my homework!

Chapter 4: NATURE Jokes

This chapter
has the best 13 funny
nature jokes

WHAT DID THE VOLCANO SAY TO HIS WIFE?

I lava you so much

WHY IS GRASS SO DANGEROUS?

Because it's full of blades.

WHY DID THE SUN GO TO SCHOOL?

To get brighter.

WHAT DID THE TREE WEAR TO THE POOL PARTY?

Swimming trunks

WHAT'S THE DIFFERENCE BETWEEN WEATHER AND CLIMATE?

You can't weather a tree,
but you can climate

HOW DO TREES GET ON THE INTERNET?

They log in.

WHY DID THE FARMER PLANT A SEED IN HIS POND?

He was trying to grow a water-melon.

WHAT DID OBI WAN KENOBI SAY TO THE TREE ON EARTH DAY?

May the Forest be with you.

WHAT IS A TREE'S FAVORITE DRINK?

Root Beer

WHAT DID ONE LIGHTENING BOLT SAY TO THE OTHER?

You're truly shocking!

WHAT DO YOU CALL IT WHEN WORMS TAKE OVER THE WORLD?

Global worming!

WHAT DO YOU CALL A FLOWER THAT RUNS ON ELECTRICITY?

A power plant!

WHAT DID THE BIG FLOWER SAY TO THE LITTLE FLOWER?

Hi bud!

Chapter 5: SPACE Jokes

This chapter has 4 funny space jokes

WHY COULDN'T THE ASTRONAUT BOOK A HOTEL ON THE MOON?

Because it was full

HOW DO YOU PAY FOR PARKING IN SPACE?

A parking meteor?

HOW DOES THE MOON CUT ITS HAIR ?

E-clipse it.

WHAT KIND OF MUSIC DO PLANETS LIKE?

Nep-tunes!

CHAPTER 6: SPORTS JOKES

This chapter has 6 funny sports jokes

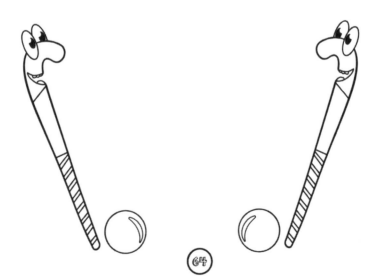

WHAT POSITION DOES A GHOST PLAY IN HOCKEY?

Ghoulie

WHAT SUPER HERO IS THE BEST AT BASEBALL?

Batman of course

IN BASEBALL, WOULD IT TAKE LONGER TO RUN FROM 1ST TO 2ND BASE OR 2ND TO 3RD BASE?

2nd to 3rd base because there's a shortstop in between.

WHICH IS FASTER? HOT OR COLD?

Hot. You can easily catch a cold.

HAVE YOU HEARD THE JOKE ABOUT THE BASEBALL?

It'll leave you in stitches.

HOW DO FOOTBALLERS STAY COOL?

They sit down
next to their fans!

Chapter 7: Pirating Jokes

This chapter has 4 funny pirating jokes

WHAT DID BLACKBEARD SAY WHEN HE TURNED 80?

"Aye, matey."

WHY IS PIRATING SO ADDICTIVE?

They say once ye lose yer first hand, ye get hooked.

HOW MUCH DOES IT COST A PIRATE TO GET HIS EARS PIERCED ?

About a buck an ear.

WHICH VEGETABLE DO PIRATES HATE THE MOST?

Leeks

Chapter 8: ANATOMY Jokes

This chapter has
6 funny Anatomy jokes

WHAT HAS TWO LEGS BUT CAN'T WALK?

A pair of pants

WHAT DID ONE EYE SAY TO THE OTHER EYE?

Between us, something smells.

WHY CAN'T YOUR NOSE BE 12 INCHES LONG?

because then it would be a foot

WHAT KIND OF HAIR DOES THE OCEAN HAVE?

Wavy

WHAT DID ONE HAT SAY TO THE OTHER?

Stay here, I'm going on ahead.

WHAT HAS ONE EYE, BUT CAN'T SEE?

A needle.

CHAPTER 9: JOKE MEDLEY

Here's a medley of 29 of our favorite jokes

WHY DO DRAGONS SLEEP DURING THE DAY?

So they can fight nights

WHY WAS IT CALLED THE DARK AGES?

Because there were lots of knights.

WHAT DO YOU A CALL A SELF DRIVING CAR THAT TAKES THE LONG WAY AROUND?

R2-detour

WHAT HAS THREE LETTERS AND STARTS WITH GAS?

A car.

WHAT AWARD
DID THE DENTIST GET?

A Plaque

WHY ARE
SATURDAY AND SUNDAY
THE STRONGEST DAYS?

The rest are just weekdays.

WHY DO SHOE STRINGS NEVER WIN A RACE?

Because they always tie!

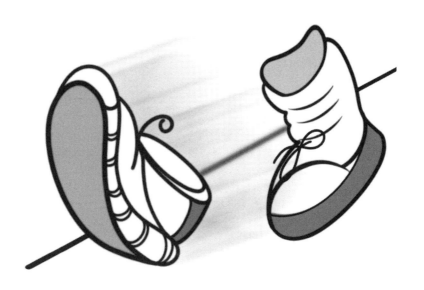

WHY DID AN OLD MAN FALL IN A WELL?

Because he couldn't see that well!

WHY COULDN'T THE BICYCLE STAND UP?

Because it was two-tired

WHAT KIND OF SHOES DO NINJAS WEAR?

Sneakers!

WHAT DO YOU CALL A MAN WITH A SHOVEL?

Doug.

WHAT'S EASY TO GET INTO, BUT HARD TO GET OUT OF?

Trouble

WHY WAS THE PICTURE SENT TO JAIL?

it was framed

WHICH ROCK GROUP HAS FOUR GUYS WHO CAN'T SING OR PLAY INSTRUMENTS?

Mount Rushmore.

WHAT BUILDING IN NEW YORK HAS THE MOST STORIES?

The public library!

WHAT DID THE TRIANGLE FEEL SORRY FOR THE CIRCLE?

Because it's pointless!

WHAT DO YOU CALL
A MONSTER WITH NO NECK?

The Lost Neck Monster.

WHAT DID ONE WALL SAY TO
THE OTHER WALL?

I'll meet you at the corner.

WHAT KIND OF MUSIC DO BALLOONS HATE?

Pop music.

WHAT GIVES YOU THE POWER TO WALK THROUGH A WALL?

A Door

WHY DOES HUMPTY DUMPTY LOVE AUTUMN?

Because he always has
a great fall.

WHERE CAN YOU FIND AN OCEAN WITHOUT WATER?

On a map!

WHICH LETTERS ARE NOT IN THE ALPHABET?

The ones in your mailbox!

IF YOU ARE AMERICAN IN THE KITCHEN AND AMERICAN IN THE BEDROOM...WHAT ARE YOU IN THE BATHROOM?

European

DID YOU HEAR ABOUT THE GUY WHO INVENTED THE KNOCK-KNOCK JOKE?

He won the "no-bell" prize.

HOW DO MINECRAFT PLAYERS CELEBRATE?

They throw block parties!

WHY DIDN'T THE LAMP SINK?

It was too light

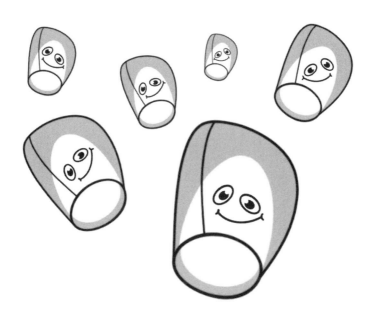

WHAT DID ONE TOILET SAY TO THE OTHER?

You look flushed!

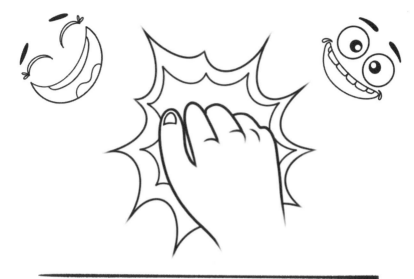

CHAPTER 10:
KNOCK KNOCK JOKES

This chapter has the best 21 funny knock-knock jokes

KNOCK KNOCK!

Who's there?

DISHES.

Dishes who?

DISHES THE POLICE. OPEN THE DOOR!

KNOCK KNOCK!

Who's there?

WOODEN SHOE.

Wooden shoe who?

WOODEN SHOE LIKE TO HEAR ANOTHER JOKE?

KNOCK KNOCK!

Who's there?

FIGS.

Figs who?

FIGS THE DOORBELL, I'VE BEEN
KNOCKING FOREVER!

KNOCK KNOCK!

Who's there?

GOLIATH.

Goliath who?

GOLIATH DOWN, YOU LOOK-ETH TIRED!

KNOCK KNOCK!

Who's there?

NANA.

Nana who?

NANA YOUR BUSINESS!

KNOCK KNOCK!

Who's there?

I AM.

I am who?

YOU DON'T KNOW WHO YOU ARE?

KNOCK KNOCK!

Who's there?

BIG INTERRUPTING COW.

Big interrupting cow who?

MOOOOOOO!

KNOCK KNOCK!

Who's there?

CANDICE.

Candice who?

CANDICE JOKE BE ANY WORSE?

KNOCK KNOCK!

Who's there?

MIKEY.

Mikey who?

MIKEY DOESN'T FIT IN THE KEY HOLE!

KNOCK KNOCK!

Who's there?

SPELL.

Spell who?

W-H-O

KNOCK KNOCK!

Who's there?

GOAT.

Goat who?

GOAT TO THE DOOR AND FIND OUT.

KNOCK KNOCK!

Who's there?

LENA.

Lena who?

LENA A LITTLE CLOSER AND I'LL TELL YOU ANOTHER JOKE!

KNOCK KNOCK!

Who's there?

RITA.

Rita who?

RITA BOOK, YOU MIGHT LEARN SOMETHING!

KNOCK KNOCK!

Who's there?

ANITA.

Anita who?

ANITA DRINK OF WATER, LET ME IN!

KNOCK KNOCK!

Who's there?

IDA.

Ida who?

I THINK IT'S PRONOUNCED IDAHO.

KNOCK KNOCK!

Who's there?

ALEX.

Alex who?

ALEX-PLAIN WHEN YOU OPEN THE DOOR!

KNOCK KNOCK!

Who's there?

ROBIN.

Robin who?

ROBIN YOU! NOW HAND OVER THE
CASH.

KNOCK KNOCK!

Who's there?

LUKE.

Luke who?

LUKE THROUGH THE KEYHOLE
AND SEE!

KNOCK KNOCK!

Who's there?

HOSP.

Horsp who?

DID YOU JUST SAY HORSE POO?

KNOCK KNOCK!

Who's there?

ANNIE.

Annie who?

ANNIE WAY YOU CAN OPEN THE DOOR?

KNOCK KNOCK!

Who's there?

ANITA.

Anita who?

ANITA GOT TO THE BATHROOM, LET ME IN!

CHAPTER 11:
ONE LINER JOKES

This chapter has the best 10
funny one liner jokes

Mountains aren't funny...
They're hill areas!

My teachers told me I'd never
amount to much because I
procrastinate so much. I told
them, "Just you wait!"

A father was cleaning his car with his son. After they're done, the son asks,
"Dad, couldn't we have done this with a sponge?"

A magician says he will disappear on the count of 3. He says
"uno, dos..." poof.
He disappeared without a tres.

My friend recently got crushed by
a pile of books, but
he's only got his shelf to blame.

I heard they put a new wing
on the middle school....
That is true,
but it still won't fly

Two muffins are sitting in an oven.
One muffin says,
"Gosh, it's hot in here!"
The other muffin says,
"Aaaah! A talking muffin!"

People think "icy" is the easiest
word to spell.
Come to think of it, I see why.

Did you hear
about the explosion at that
french cheese factory?
All that was left was de brie.

The past, present, and future
walked into a bar.
It was tense.